THE BAPTIST PRIMER

an illustrated introduction to baptist history and distinctives

NATHAN G. DEATRICK

illustrated by Marilyn Stevens

Nathan Deatrick planted and is pastor of the Crossroads Baptist Church in Columbus, NC. He and his wife, Jenny, have four children: Emalyn Joyce, Audrey Elizabeth, Judson Clarke, and Elaina Ann. Judson is named after Adoniram Judson, the first Baptist missionary sent from American soil, and after Dr. John Clarke, one of the first Baptist pastors on American soil. Nathan is part of the third generation of Baptist pastors in his family. Second only to his personal, daily Bible study, his study of Baptist history has done more than any other influence to shape his life and his love for local church ministry.

Marilyn Stevens, a local artist in Charleston, South Carolina, is the wife of a Baptist pastor and grandmother of six grandchildren. She was born in Ravenswood, West Virginia, grew up on a dairy farm in Ohio, then lived many years in California before moving to the East coast. Artwork has been a big part of Marilyn's life as she has labored together with her husband in the ministry providing drawings and paintings for children's stories, songs, object lessons and many other doors of opportunity. Marilyn also does watercolor paintings of the Charleston historic sites and sells her prints to help with missions. She gives God all the credit for any talent she has and desires to use it for His glory alone.

First published in 2006 by Nathan Deatrick in Shelby, NC. Published in 2011 by Striving Together Publications, a ministry of Lancaster Baptist Church, Lancaster, CA 93535. Striving Together Publications is committed to providing tried, trusted, and proven books that will further equip local churches to carry out the Great Commission. Your comments and suggestions are valued.

Striving Together Publications
4020 E. Lancaster Blvd.
Lancaster, CA 93535
800.201.7748

Layout and design by Pixel Graphic Design Studio
Cover design by Andrew Hutchens

ISBN 978-1-59894-158-6
Printed in Canada

To the Parent or Teacher...

The study of history is vital to the education of children. If you doubt this, then take note of the subtle reconstruction of American history over the last one hundred years, and you will realize that the history and future of a people are inseparably linked. A people that forget their history jeopardize their future and squander their present. History is the compass point which keeps a people on track for the future. If you would change the course of a people's future, you must alter the record of their history. It is incumbent upon every generation to educate the next generation on that inseparable link between the past and the future. Our history as Baptists is even more vital to the education of our children. For it is the record of where we began, how we got to where we are, and why we are what we are in relation to our Lord, His church, and His Word, not just our country.

The formative years of childhood provide the greatest opportunity to educate the minds and hearts of the coming generation. Educators with liberal, evil agendas realize this. Bible-believing Baptists, with righteous cause, should realize no less. It should grieve us to think of teenagers, young adults, and even older adults in our churches being ignorant of our Baptist history and distinctives. The mind of a child is an inquisitive mind. An inquisitive mind is a fertile mind, which in turn is a moldable mind. If we are to educate our people on a subject of such incalculable worth, we are foolish to wait until those fertile days of childhood are passed. I am convinced in my soul that we must thoroughly verse our children in the history and distinctives of Baptists. There is no reason, nor time to wait!

Because of this conviction, I have been burdened to write this little book, *The Baptist Primer*. It is the result of more than five years of study. When I began this study, I had no idea that it would end in a book, much less an illustrated children's book. Much which targets the advanced reader has been written, and is being written on Baptist history, but precious little has been written for our children.

I have structured *The Baptist Primer* in the mold of the school primers of America's early days and have added a touch of the Hebrew method which used the alphabet and poetry to aid the memory. The illustrations will help to engrave more indelibly the truth of the poem upon the tables of a child's heart. Along with the poetry and pictures, a third and final ingredient will enhance the success of this book. That ingredient is you, the parent or teacher! For your part I have included several tools which will assist you in introducing children to Baptist history and distinctives. At the bottom of the pages which teach one of the Baptist distinctives you will find a memory verse which is a biblical support for that distinctive. At the bottom of a page which teaches a golden nugget of Baptist history you will find a brief narrative on that historical event, as well as a fitting memory verse. A glossary of terms is included at the end of the book for the words which are italicized in the text. This will allow you to easily define these more difficult words to children as the book is being read. Furthermore, the resource guide at the end of the book provides even more scriptural support for the Baptist distinctives and more suggested reading on the subject of our heritage.

I leave you with two verses of Scripture for meditation. "If the foundations be destroyed, what can the righteous do?" (Psalm 11:3). "Remove not the ancient landmark, which thy fathers have set" (Proverbs 22:28).

Nathan G. Deatrick
Shelby, North Carolina

A is for our **Authority**, the Bible,
Given to us by God,
To teach us and to lead us
In all the paths we *trod*.

"All scripture is given by *inspiration* of God, and
is profitable for *doctrine*, for *reproof*, for *correction*,
for *instruction* in righteousness."
2 TIMOTHY 3:16

B is for **Believer Priests**
Who need not through men pray,
But they can go alone themselves
Before God's throne each day.

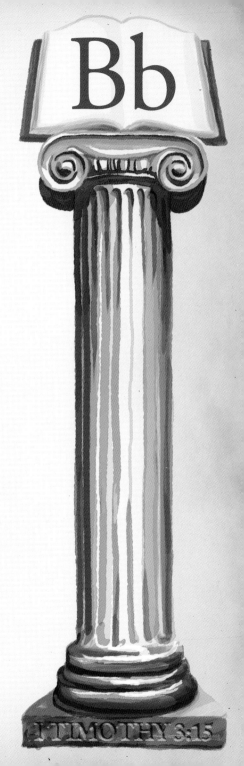

"Let us therefore come boldly unto the
throne of grace, that we may obtain mercy,
and find grace to help in time of need."
HEBREWS 4:16

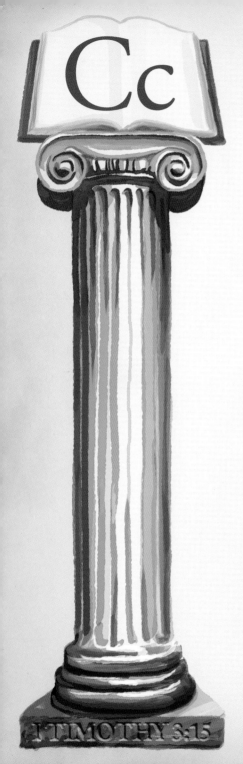

C is for **Church Membership**
Only for those born again.
They promise to each other
To keep themselves from sin.

"And the Lord added to the church daily
such as should be saved."
ACTS 2:47B

D is for the **Discipline**
 Of church members living in sin.
In love we gently correct them
 And bring them back again.

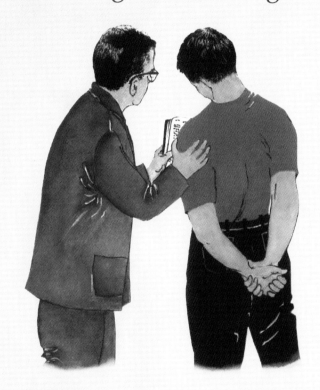

"Brethren, if any of you do err from the truth, and one *convert* him; Let him know, that he which converteth the sinner from the error of his way shall save a soul from death, and shall hide a multitude of sins."
JAMES 5:19–20

Dd

I TIMOTHY 3:15

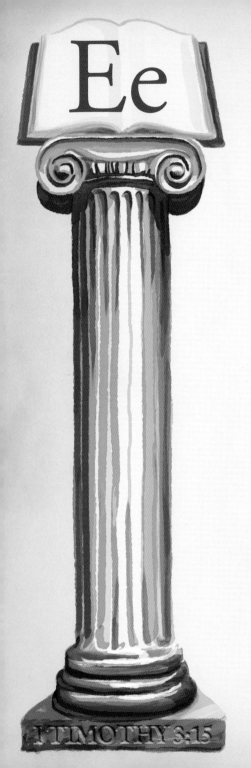

E is for the **Enemies**
    Of Baptist truths of old.
Father, please, forgive them,
    And help us to be bold.

It is estimated that some 50,000,000 people were martyred by the Roman Catholic Church during the *Dark Ages*.[1] Most of these were slain simply for the crime of having been an *Anabaptist*. These are saints "Of whom the world was not worthy" (HEBREWS 11:38).

F is for the **Freedom**
  To worship by God's plan,
Not by force of government
  Or by the law of man.

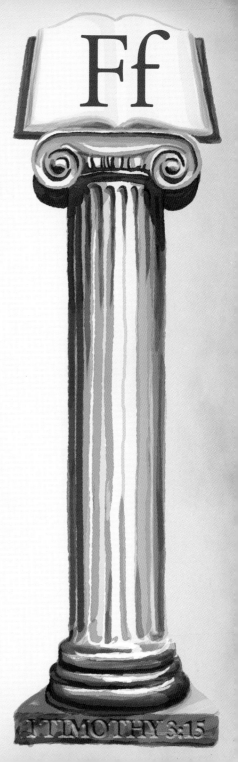

On July 9, 1663, John Clarke, pastor of the Baptist church in Newport, Rhode Island, obtained a *charter* from Charles II, King of England, which granted absolute religious liberty for the colony of Rhode Island. Along with Roger Williams, he had worked for eleven years to gain this permission. This date marks the birth of religious liberty in America. Never was it more true that "The king's heart is in the hand of the Lord, as the rivers of water: he turneth it withersoever he will" (Proverbs 21:1).

I TIMOTHY 3:15

G is for Baptist church **Government**,
Which for America did provide,
In the eyes of Thomas Jefferson,
A faithful, working guide.

During his frequent visits to a small Baptist church near his home, Thomas Jefferson was impressed by how Baptist churches governed themselves. He felt that Baptist principles of church government would be valuable to the new American government, too.[2] Traces of these principles are not difficult to find in America's founding documents. Thomas Jefferson saw to it! Truly, every Baptist church should strive to "Let all things be done decently and in order" (1 CORINTHIANS 14:40).

H is for Baptist **History**;
　　From the Bible we can know
　　Not just where we came from,
　　But where we ought to go.

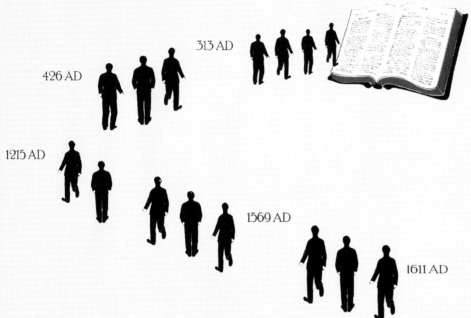

426 AD

313 AD

1215 AD

1569 AD

1611 AD

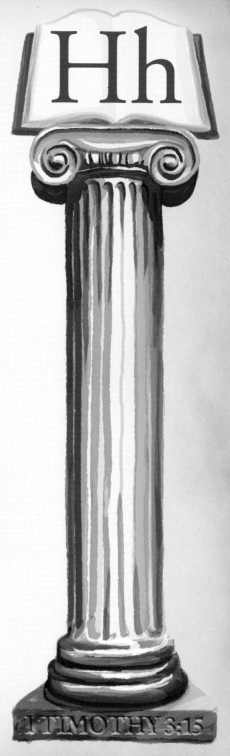

Hh

1 TIMOTHY 3:15

An open minded study of Baptist history reveals an obvious relationship of Baptist believers back to the time of the apostles. Even many Baptist enemies have observed this. However, because a connection of believers who have held Baptist principles may be traced throughout history does not make us right.[3] Likeness and obedience to the Bible makes us right. The Apostle Paul showed that truth would produce a continual succession of believers when he said, "The things that thou hast heard of me among many witnesses, the same commit thou to faithful men, who shall be able to teach others also" (2 TIMOTHY 2:2).

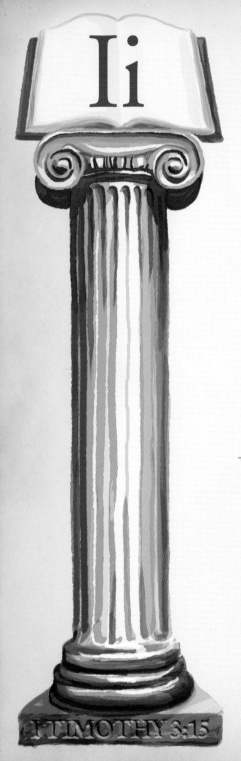

I is for **Immersion**,
    For believers only.
In the waters of baptism
    We are baptized wholly.

"Then they that gladly received his word were baptized" (ACTS 2:41).
"The eunuch said, See, here is water; what doth hinder me to be
baptized? And Philip said, If thou believest with all thine heart, thou
mayest. And he answered and said, I believe that Jesus Christ is the
Son of God. And he commanded the chariot to stand still: and they
went down both into the water, both Philip and the eunuch; and he
baptized him" (ACTS 8:36–38).

I TIMOTHY 3:15

J is for Mr. **Judson** and Mr. Rice,
Who sailed to foreign field,
To preach the Gospel story
To sinners needing to be healed.

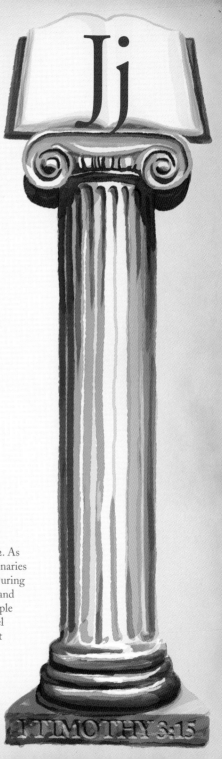

Adoniram Judson and Luther Rice were not Baptists when they sailed as missionaries to Burma in 1812. As Congregationalists, who believed in baby baptism, they knew that they would be meeting Baptist missionaries when they arrived on the field, and they must be prepared to defend their position against the Baptists. During their long ocean voyage—on separate ships from one another—they had many hours to study the Bible, and became convinced by the Word of God that, in fact, the Baptists were right! Baptism is only for saved people and is to be done by immersion. In obedience to the Scripture they were baptized in a little Baptist chapel in Calcutta, India, while waiting to go to Burma. Once they became Baptists, they could no longer accept support money from the *Congregational* churches of America. Mr. Rice returned home in 1813 to rally the Baptists of America to the cause of foreign missions, so that Mr. Judson and many other missionaries could preach the Gospel in Burma and around the world. The Baptists of America met the challenge and in them were echoed the words of the apostle Paul when he said, "For from you sounded out the word of the Lord not only in Macedonia and Achaia, but also in every place your faith to God-ward is spread abroad; so that we need not to speak any thing" (1 THESSALONIANS 1:8).

I TIMOTHY 3:15

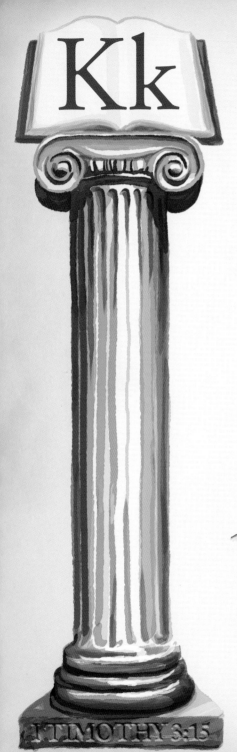

I TIMOTHY 3:15

K is for the **Keeping**,
By the power of God,
Of those who've called on Jesus
And trusted in His Word.

"And I give unto them eternal life; and they shall
never perish, neither shall any man pluck them out of
my hand. My Father, which gave them me, is greater
than all; and no man is able to pluck them out of my
Father's hand. I and my Father are one."

JOHN 10:28–30

L is for each **Local Church**;
Independent from the rest
To love and serve the Saviour
In the way that it sees best.

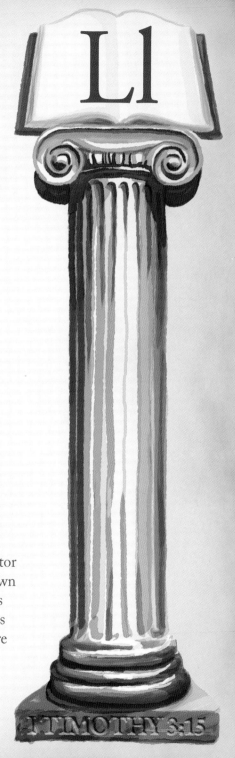

In the Bible, every local church was responsible for *ordaining* its own pastor (TITUS 1:5); taking care of its own pastor (1 TIMOTHY 5:17); choosing its own deacons (ACTS 6:1–6); adding its own members (ACTS 2:41); correcting its own members (2 THESSALONIANS 3:14–15); expelling unrepentant members (1 CORINTHIANS 5:4–5, 11); determining correctness of doctrine by Scripture (ACTS 17:11; GALATIANS 1:8); sending its own missionaries (ACTS 13:1–3); collecting its own offerings (1 CORINTHIANS 16:1–2); disbursing those fferings (PHILIPPIANS 4:14–18); helping its own needy (1 TIMOTHY 5:3); and baptizing and teaching its own converts (MATTHEW 28:18–20).

1 TIMOTHY 3:15

Mm

I TIMOTHY 3:15

M is for the **Martyrs**;
  So many of Baptist beliefs;
  Who gladly suffered for Christ's sake,
  Instead of being released.

"Blessed are they which are persecuted for righteousness' sake: for theirs is the kingdom of heaven. Blessed are ye, when men shall revile you, and persecute you, and shall say all manner of evil against you falsely, for my sake. Rejoice and be exceeding glad: for great is your reward in heaven: for so persecuted they the prophets which were before you" (MATTHEW 5:10–12). "Others were tortured, not accepting deliverance; that they might obtain a better resurrection" (HEBREWS 11:35).

N is for the different **Names**
    By which our enemies made us known;
But not until the early 1600s,
    Did we make the Baptist name our own.

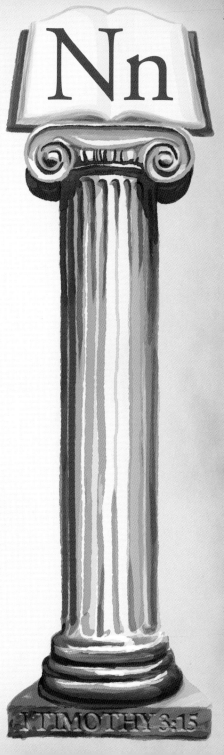

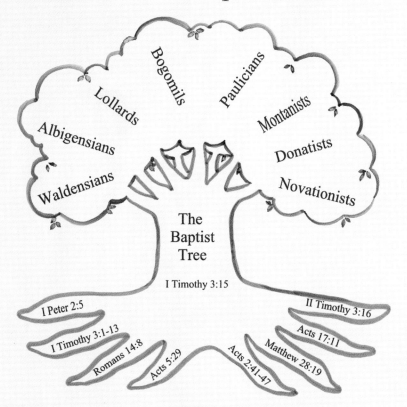

Baptists have been known by many different names throughout history. Luke records that "the disciples were called Christians first in Antioch" (Acts 11:26). Many more names were to follow, and most all of these were given to believers by their enemies. Only in the early 1600s did they finally call themselves by the name Baptist. No matter the names they have been called, they were no less Baptist.

Oo

O is for two church **Officers**;
The pastor and the deacon;
The one to lead; the one to serve,
And both to be a *beacon*.

"Remember them which have the rule over you, who
have spoken unto you the word of God: whose faith
follow, considering the end of their *conversation*."
HEBREWS 13:7

1 TIMOTHY 3:15

P is for the **Promise**
Our Lord made long ago,
That nothing can destroy His church,
Not even Hell below!

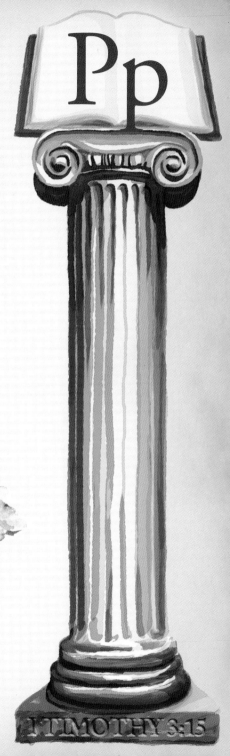

"Upon this rock I will build my church; and the
gates of hell shall not *prevail* against it."
Matthew 16:18

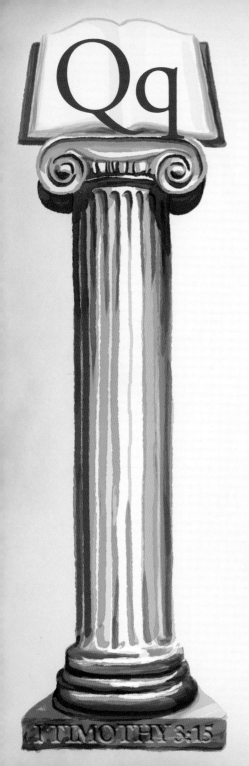

I TIMOTHY 3:15

Q is for the **Quality**
  Of Baptists world-wide,
Who stood for truth and loved the right,
  When they had no place to hide.

"Wherefore, seeing we also are *compassed* about with so
great a *cloud* of witnesses, let us lay aside every weight,
and the sin which doth so easily *beset* us, and let us run
with patience the race that is set before us, Looking
unto Jesus the author and finisher of our faith."

HEBREWS 12:1–2

R is for **Rhode Island**;
Where John Clarke,
Roger Williams and more
First started Baptist churches
On America's eastern shore.

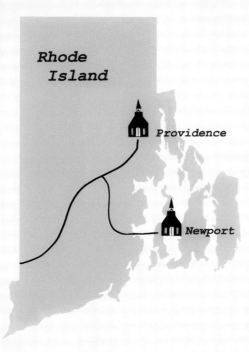

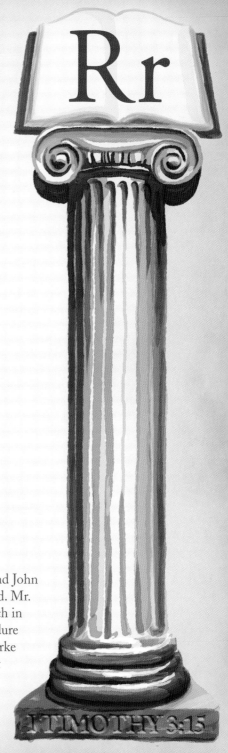

The first two Baptist churches on American soil were started by Roger Williams and John Clarke in the year 1638.[4] Both churches were founded in the colony of Rhode Island. Mr. William's church was established in the town of Providence and Mr. Clarke's church in the town of Newport. Although Williams soon became a "*Seeker*," and did not endure as a Baptist, his labors on behalf of absolute religious liberty are priceless. John Clarke must rightly be recognized as the Father of Baptists in America and America's first Baptist pastor. Pastor Clarke was a man who heeded Paul's admonition to "Take heed to thyself, and unto the doctrine; continue in them: for in doing this thou shalt both save thyself, and them that hear thee" (1 TIMOTHY 4:16).

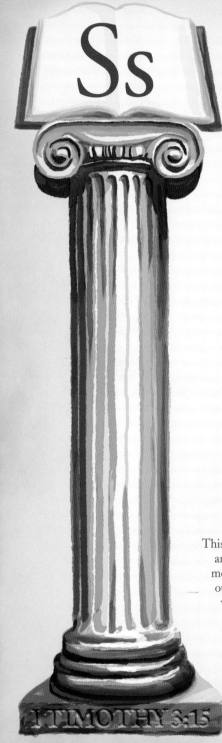

I TIMOTHY 3:15

S is for **Separation**
Of our church and every member
From *apostasy* and worldliness
Unto our Great Redeemer.

This picture represents the emblem of the ancient group of believers called the Waldensians. They are some of the most famous of our Baptist ancestors. The Latin phrase *Lux Lucet in Tenebris* means "The Light Shineth in the Darkness." One of the marks of Bible believing Baptists and our ancestors in the faith is that we have been recognized by our separation from apostasy and worldly living. We are like a light shining brightly in a sin-darkened world. The Apostle Paul was very clear that separated living would always mark godly believers when he said, "For ye were sometimes darkness, but now are ye light in the Lord: walk as children of light: (For the fruit of the Spirit is in all goodness and righteousness and truth;) Proving what is acceptable unto the Lord. And have no fellowship with the unfruitful works of darkness, but rather reprove them. For it is a shame even to speak of those things which are done of them in secret. But all things that are reproved are made manifest by the light: for whatsoever doth make manifest is light. Wherefore he saith, Awake thou that sleepest, and arise from the dead, and Christ shall give thee light" (EPHESIANS 5:8–14).

T is for **Two Church Ordinances**;
　　Baptism and Lord's Table.
We follow them in obedience,
　　Not just if we feel able.

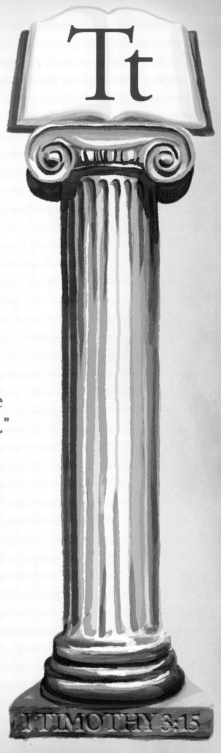

"This do in
remembrance
of me..."

The so-called *sacraments* of the Catholic Church, as well as the
practices of other churches of different beliefs, cannot rightly be called
ordinances. Baptism and the Lord's Table are the only two ordinances
given by the Lord to His church. They are to be a continuing part of
a local church's life. Baptism is commanded in Acts 2:38. The Lord's
Table is commanded in 1 Corinthians 11:24–25.

I TIMOTHY 3:15

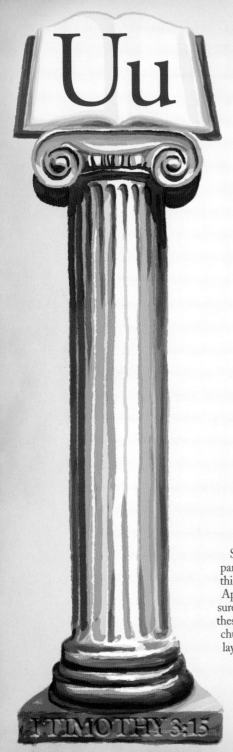

I TIMOTHY 3:15

U is for the **Unbroken Line of Baptists**
Outside the Church of Rome,
Who pass to us the torch of truth
To be carried on and on.

Study the ancient Baptist groups, and a major truth becomes apparent. They never had any part in the Roman Catholic Church. These ancient peoples may not have been perfect, but one thing is for sure; they were not *Protestants* who came out of the Church of Rome. They, like the Apostle Peter, could say, "We have not followed *cunningly* devised *fables*…We have also a more sure word of prophecy; whereunto ye do well that ye take heed" (2 PETER 1:16, 19). The loyalty of these ancient groups rested in the Word of God and not the traditions and fables of a man-made church. Consider carefully the words of the great Baptist pastor, C. H. Spurgeon, spoken at the laying of the cornerstone of the Metropolitan Tabernacle on April 2, 1861. "We believe Baptists are the original Christians. We did not commence our existence at the Reformation, we were Reformers before Luther or Calvin were born; we never came from the Church of Rome, for we were never in it, but we have an unbroken line up to the apostles themselves. We have always existed from the very days of Christ, and our principles, sometimes veiled and forgotten, like a river which may travel underground for a little season, have always had honest and holy adherents."

V is for the **Valleys**
Where Waldensians did flee;
Until from persecution
They would finally be free.

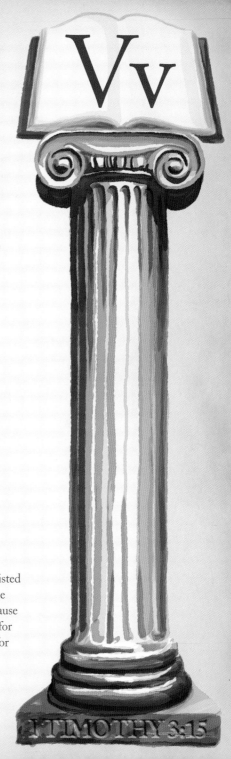

Godly man that he was, Peter Waldo was not the founder of the Waldensians. Waldensians existed
long before Peter Waldo ever left the Catholic Church in the late twelfth century.[5] The name
Waldensian means "people of the valley." Why were the Waldensians people of the valley? Because
it was in the valleys of the European Alps that these Baptist folks lived, worshipped, and died for
Christ's sake. Many ancient Baptist believers of various names fled into the valleys of the Alps for
refuge during the persecutions of the Dark Ages. What were they to find in those valleys but a
people believing just as they did, only called by the name Waldensians. Call them what you
will, they were Baptists by the Book! The Waldensians believed the words of the Apostle
John in Revelation 12:6, "And the woman fled into the wilderness, where she hath a place
prepared of God," well illustrated their experiences as sufferers for Christ's sake.

I TIMOTHY 3:15

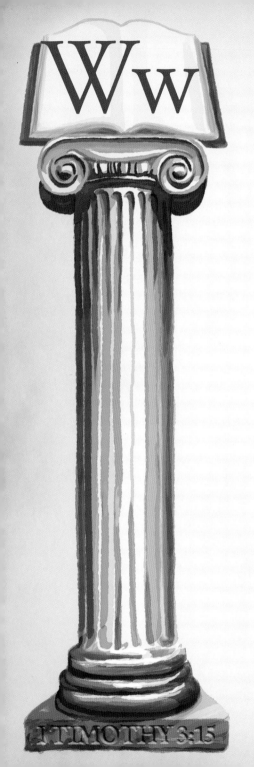

I TIMOTHY 3:15

W is for the **Witness**
Baptist saints have been;
Spreading forth the Gospel;
Inviting folks to Heaven.

"But ye shall receive power, after that the Holy Ghost
is come upon you: and ye shall be witnesses unto me
both in Jerusalem, and in all Judea, and in Samaria,
and unto the uttermost part of the earth."
ACTS 1:8

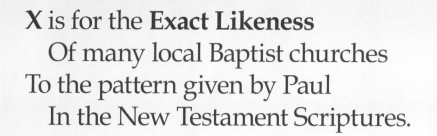

X is for the **Exact Likeness**
  Of many local Baptist churches
To the pattern given by Paul
  In the New Testament Scriptures.

The testimony of the *liberal* German *linguist*, Wilhelm Gesenius, is one of many which reveals the likeness of local Baptist churches to the New Testament pattern. When he heard the description of a Baptist church, Wilhelm Gesenius exclaimed, "How exactly like the Primitive Churches!"[6] Numerous other non-Baptists have said similar things, but the testimony of a liberal does not make a Baptist church right. Likeness to the Bible makes a Baptist church right. A Baptist church which is patterned after the Bible realizes that it cannot change the truth, or update the truth. Truth is timeless. A biblical Baptist church is simply "the *pillar* and *ground* of the truth" (1 TIMOTHY 3:15).

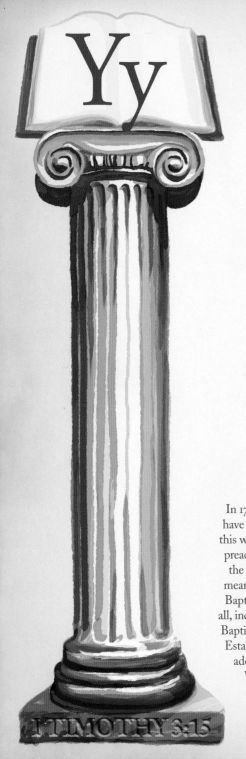

Y is for **Your Choice**
To become a Baptist or not.
We will not make you be one;
We will not and cannot.

In 1784, Patrick Henry, a great friend of Baptists and religious liberty, supported a bill that would have required all Virginians to pay a tax to support the denomination of their choice.[7] He believed this would be a relief to the persecuted Baptists; 44 Baptist preachers had been jailed in Virginia for preaching without a license from the state. Before this time, all men were taxed for the support of the *Episcopalian* Church alone, no matter their religious beliefs. But now, according to the well-meaning plan of Patrick Henry, even the Baptists could be supported by tax dollars. However, the Baptists disagreed and argued that tax dollars should not be used to support any denomination at all, including themselves. No one should be forced by the government to support religion. Virginia's Baptists, with the help of James Madison, saw the bill defeated in 1785. Thomas Jefferson's Bill for Establishing Religious Freedom became law in Virginia in 1786,[8] and the First Amendment was added to the United States Constitution in 1791, largely through the efforts of John Leland and Virginia Baptists. Baptists will not make a man support them or become one! Baptists learned the principle of religious freedom from none other than the Lord Jesus. As he overlooked the city of Jerusalem, He said, "How often would I have gathered thy children together, even as a hen gathereth her chickens under her wings, and ye would not" (MATTHEW 23:37).

Z is for the **Zeal**
　　Of Pastor Shubal Stearns,
　Who started Baptist churches,
　　So men to Christ would turn.

One of the most inspiring Baptists of American history is Pastor Shubal Stearns. In 1755, Shubal Stearns arrived in the rough-hewn wilderness of North Carolina and started the Sandy Creek Baptist Church near present-day Greensboro. Within a few short years, the congregation of that church grew from 16 members to 606 members. By 1772, the Sandy Creek Baptist Church had started forty-two other Baptist churches, not only in North Carolina, but also in Virginia, South Carolina, Georgia, Kentucky and Tennessee. One author estimates that within two generations over 5,000 Baptist churches sprung from the Sandy Creek Baptist Church.[9] The Baptist churches of these six states formed the base from which Baptists would move westward through the *Louisiana Purchase* planting thousands more Baptist churches. The accomplishments of Shubal Stearns are breathtaking, but in his eyes he was simply following Christ and would say with the Apostle Paul, "Be ye followers of me, even as I also am of Christ" (1 CORINTHIANS 11:1). All Baptist parents should see to it that this man is one of their children's heroes!

GLOSSARY OF TERMS
(Listed in Alphabetical Order)

Anabaptist
The general name given to most ancient Baptist groups. It combines the Greek words *ana* meaning "again" and *baptidzo* meaning "to baptize." The word was used by Roman Catholics and Protestants, who baptized infants, to refer to those who were baptized again after having been baptized as a baby. Almost without exception, all Baptist groups have rejected the name Anabaptist, because they say that infant baptism is not baptism at all. Biblical baptism is by immersion and only for those who are old enough to have personally received the Lord Jesus Christ as Saviour.

Apostasy
The act of departing from or revolting against the truth of God's Word. Biblically, a person who has apostatized against God and His Word was never genuinely saved in the first place (1 John 2:19).

Beacon
A bright light which guides the way (1 Timothy 4:12).

Beset
To ensnare or trap someone or something (James 1:13–16).

Burma
The old name for the present day country of Myanmar which is bordered by China on the north, Thailand and Laos on the east, India and Bangladesh on the west, and the Indian Ocean on the south.

Charter
A legal document which gives rights or privileges to those to whom it is granted.

Cloud
This use of the word "cloud" pictures the Old Testament saints surrounding New Testament believers as a body of witnesses unified in their faith and testimony.

Compassed
To be surrounded by someone or something.

Congregational
The Congregational Church broke away from the Church of England in 1602 as "Independents." The Church of England was nothing more than the Roman Catholic Church with a King instead of a Pope. In many ways the Congregational Church is the Church of England without a King. The Congregational Church sprinkles infants and does not require a saved church membership. Ironically, when Congregationalists arrived in America, they established a state church and persecuted dissenters. This was the very thing they themselves had fled in England.

Conversation
This does not refer to the words which come from a man's mouth as he talks to others, but is an old English word referring to the manner of life a man lives.

Convert
To turn about or to turn again (Galatians 6:1).

Correction
What one must do to get right with God (Psalm 119:9).

Cunningly
Sneaky or crafty.

The Dark Ages
The period of time between the year 426 AD and the Reformation wherein the Roman Catholic Church hid from the known world the light of God's Word. The people, and eventually even the priests themselves, were not allowed access to the Bible, but were only taught the Roman Catholic traditions and interpretations of the Bible. It is no wonder this period of time has come to be known as the Dark Ages.

Doctrine
The teaching of what is right in the eyes of God (Micah 6:8).

Episcopalian
The American branch of the Church of England (Anglican).

Fables
A myth or make-believe, pretend story.

Ground
The foundation which supported an object. It also refers to a public platform from which official declarations were made.

Immersion

The act of plunging or fully sinking a person into water. This is what the Greek word *baptidzo* literally means. It is improper to imply that the English word baptize can refer to sprinkling or pouring.

Inspiration

God had the writers of Scripture write down the exact words He wanted written (2 Peter 1:21).

Instruction

What one must do to stay right with God (Psalm 119:9–10).

Liberal

A person who does not believe the Bible is the literal, inspired Word of God, but believes that it is open to critical interpretation. He believes the Bible is only a record of man's ideas about God and not God's revelation of Himself to man. He does not believe in the supernatural parts of the Bible. To him the prophecies contained in the Bible were recorded after the event they foretold, not before. He believes the miracles of the Bible were the result of the writer's imagination.

Linguist

A person who is an expert in the study of different languages.

Louisiana Purchase

This purchase was made by the U.S. from France in 1803, when Thomas Jefferson was president. The Louisiana Territory not only included the state of Louisiana, but also took in Arkansas, Missouri, Iowa, Kansas, Nebraska, and portions of New Mexico, Texas, Wyoming, North Dakota, South Dakota, Montana, Oklahoma, Minnesota, and Colorado. These states make up the middle third of the continental United States and cover 828,000 square miles. The purchase price was $15,000,000.

Ordaining

The act of a local church when it officially authorizes a man to the ministry of pastor or deacon. However, a man is only ordained by a local church after his giftedness has been recognized and proven, and he has demonstrated he meets the qualifications of Scripture in 1 Timothy 3:1–13 and Titus 1:6–9.

Ordinances

A permanent rule of action established by an authority. A local church's authority is the Word of the Lord Jesus Christ.

Pillar

The mast of a ship on which all the sails hung, so that the ship could be propelled by the wind. It also refers to sign posts upon which public notices were hung.

Prevail

To overpower or to have power over someone or something with the implication of causing defeat.

Protestant

Generally describes those denominations that protested against the Roman Catholic Church during the time of the Reformation. The founders of these denominations thought the Roman Church was a "good church gone bad" and thought to reform it by their protests. When their protests were ignored, they broke away and started their own churches, but kept what they wanted of the Roman Church's doctrine and practice.

Reproof

A warning against what is not right in the eyes of God (Psalm 19:11).

Sacraments

A religious work which is thought necessary to salvation and is commanded by Catholic and Protestant churches.

Seeker

A person who believes he is on a quest for the truth, but he has not fully found it yet.

Trod

An old English word for the act of walking.

RESOURCES

This acrostic of the word "BAPTISTS" is helpful in remembering the Distinctives.

Biblical Authority
Joshua 1:8; 2 Samuel 23:1–2; Psalm 19:1–14; 33:11; Psalm 119; Isaiah 55:11; Matthew 4:4–11; 5:18; 1 Corinthians 2:4–5; 1 Peter 1:21–25; 2 Peter 1:16–21

Autonomy of the Local Church
Matthew 18:15–17; Acts 13:1–3; Acts 17:11; 1 Corinthians 5:4–5, 11; 16:1–2; Galatians 1:8; Philippians 4:14–18; 2 Thessalonians 3:14–15; 1 Timothy 3:15; 5:9; 5:17; Titus 1:5

Priesthood of the Believer
Romans 8:17; Ephesians 2:6, 19; 1 Peter 2:4–10; 1 John 4:1–2; Revelation 1:6; 5:10

Two Church Officers
Acts 6:1–7; 20:28; Philippians 1:1; 1 Timothy 3:1–13; Titus 1:6–9; 1 Peter 5:1–4

Individual Soul Liberty
Matthew 23:37; Romans 14:1–23; 1 Corinthians 8:1–13; Galatians 5:12–26; Colossians 2:16–22

Saved Church Membership
Acts 2:41, 47; 5:14; 11:24; 16:5; Romans 14:1; 1 Corinthians 5:1–13

Two Church Ordinances
Matthew 3:6, 16; 26:26–29; 28:19; Mark 1:5, 9–10; 14:22–25; Luke 22:17–20; John 3:23; Acts 2:41; 8:38–39; Romans 6:1–5; 1 Corinthians 11:23–26

Separation of Church and State
Proverbs 24:21; Jeremiah 29:7; Matthew 22:17–22; Acts 5:29; Romans 13:1–7; 1 Timothy 2:1–3; Titus 3:2; 1 Peter 2:13–17

The following list of books is not exhaustive, but will assist in learning more about Baptist History. Listing these books here does not mean the author is in total agreement with the perspective of the author or the content of the book. By referring to the bibliographies of these books, even more resources can be discovered. I have only included the Title and Author, but this should be sufficient information for locating some of these books should you desire. The publish dates on several of these books are old, but reprints are available.

A General History of the Baptist Denomination by David Benedict
A Glorious Church by Mike Gass
A History of the Baptists by John T. Christian
A History of the Baptists by Thomas Armitage
A History of the Donatists by David Benedict
A Short History of the Baptists by Henry C. Vedder
America in Crimson Red by James R. Beller
Miller's Church History by Andrew Miller
Ray's Baptist Succession by David Burcham Ray
The Baptist Encyclopedia by William Cathcart
The Baptist Heritage by Leon McBeth
The Bible Makes Us Baptists by Mary E. Bamford
The Book of Martyrs by John Foxe
The Collegiate Baptist History Workbook by James R. Beller
The Ecclesiastical History of the Ancient Churches of the Piedmont and of the Albigenses by Peter Allix
The Little Baptist by J. M. Martin
The History of the Christian Church by Philip Schaff
The Martyr's Mirror by Thieleman J. Van Braght
The Pilgrim Church by E. H. Broadbent
The Trail of Blood by J. M. Carroll
This Day in Baptist History by Thompson and Cummins

ENDNOTES

1. Carroll, J.M. *The Trail of Blood*. (Lexington, KY: Ashland Avenue Baptist Church, 1931.), 14.

2. Armitage, Thomas. *A History of the Baptists*. 2 vols. (New York: Bryan, Taylor & Co., 1890.), II, 733–734.

3. There are Baptists, often called "Landmark Baptists or Baptist Briders," who believe and teach that their authority and validity of existence rests in the fact that they can trace a visible succession of individual churches all the way back to NT times from church to church to church. They attempt to trace their right to exist horizontally through other churches exactly like them. This really is an impossible endeavor. It must be understood that the right of a local church to exist comes vertically from the Lord, only as that individual church is patterned after the Bible. As that church departs from the Bible, it forfeits its identity as a scriptural, NT local church. When Paul said to Timothy in 2 Timothy 2:2, "And the things that thou hast heard of me…the same commit thou to faithful men…," his focus was on a succession of the doctrines and principles of Scripture. These principles were to be taught to generation after generation of Bible believers. Local churches, made up of believers, holding to the Baptistic principles of NT Scripture, have always existed in history; Jesus promised this in Matthew 16:18. However, at times, because of persecution, destruction of their writings or other factors, they have been difficult to trace. Any visible connection of Baptist believers is wonderful evidence that Jesus has kept His promise! This author holds to the "Succession of Baptist Principles" view of Baptist history. The connection of Baptistic believers in history is consequential to their holding the Baptistic principles of the Bible. The author would add that he rejects, as unbiblical, illogical, and untenable, the so-called English Baptist Descent theory of Baptist heritage, which argues that Baptists are Protestants which came out of the Reformation.

4. Beller, James R. *America in Crimson Red*. (Arnold, MO: Prairie Fire Press, 2004.), 30–33.

5. Christian, John T. *A History of the Baptists*. 2 vols. (Texarkana, AR: Bogard Press, 1922.), I, 69–82.

6. Armitage, Thomas. *A History of the Baptists*. 2 vols. (New York: Bryan, Taylor & Co., 1890.) I, 149.

7. Christian, John T. *A History of the Baptists*. 2 vols. (Texarkana, AR: Bogard Press, 1922.), II, 270–273.

8. Dawson, Joseph M. *Baptists and the American Republic*. (Nashville, TN: Broadman Press, 1956.), 103–107.

9. Beller, James R. *The Coming Destruction of the Baptist People*. (St. Louis, MO: Prairie Fire Press, 2005.), 40.